I0500622

Congressional
Research
Service

Presidential Appointee Positions Requiring Senate Confirmation and Committees Handling Nominations

Christopher M. Davis
Analyst on Congress and the Legislative Process

Jerry W. Mansfield
Information Research Specialist

November 15, 2012

Congressional Research Service

7-5700

www.crs.gov

RL30959

Summary

As part of the process of making an appointment to an advice and consent position, the President usually submits a nomination to the Senate. The Senate's executive clerk, acting on behalf of the Senate's presiding officer, refers the nomination to the appropriate committee or committees on the day it is received. When making a referral, the executive clerk is guided by Senate Rule XXV, which establishes the subject matter under the purview of each committee and directs that "all proposed legislation, messages, petitions, memorials, and other matters relating primarily to [those] subjects" be referred to that committee. The executive clerk is also guided by precedents set by prior referrals and by standing orders and unanimous consent (UC) agreements adopted by the Senate pertaining to the referral of nominations.

Most nominations are referred to one committee. For some positions, a nomination or series of nominations to a position are referred to more than one committee, pursuant to a standing order, a UC agreement, or a statutory provision. A nomination may be jointly or sequentially referred to multiple committees. Joint referral has generally occurred when more than one committee has had a claim to jurisdiction over the subject matter related to the position. Under joint referral, the committees receive the nomination simultaneously and may consider it concurrently. All committees to which a nomination is referred must report it to the full Senate or be discharged from its further consideration before it may be considered on the floor. Sequential referral has generally occurred when one committee has had predominant jurisdiction over the subject matter related to the position, but other committees have had a claim as well. Under this process, a nomination is referred to the committee with predominant jurisdiction first and is then sequentially referred to additional committees. Consideration of subsequent referrals can be subject to a time limit after which the committee or committees without primary jurisdiction are automatically discharged from further consideration of the nomination. Certain nominations or categories of nominations are subject to a potentially more expedited Senate consideration pursuant to a standing order adopted in the 112th Congress.

This report identifies, by Senate committee, presidentially appointed positions requiring Senate confirmation based on referrals as of the date of passage of S. 679, which became P.L. 112-166 on August 10, 2012. This public law removed numerous presidentially appointed positions from the advice and consent process for relevant U.S. Senate committees. A complete list of the presidentially appointed positions that no longer require Senate confirmation may be found in the Appendix of this report. For each committee list, positions are categorized as full- or part-time and then grouped by department or agency. Where nominations have been referred to more than one committee, the organizations and titles are noted under each of the committees to which the nominations were referred. The lists also include the lengths of fixed terms, where applicable. Some commissions, councils, and other multi-member entities are required, by their enabling statutes, to maintain political balance in some way. This is noted in parentheses where applicable.

The information provided in this report was compiled from the Senate nominations database of the Legislative Information System available to the congressional community at http://www.congress.gov/nomis (the public database is http://thomas.loc.gov/home/nomis.html), data on departmental and agency websites, telephone conversations with agency officials, and the *United States Code*. For related information, see CRS Report RL31980, *Senate Consideration of Presidential Nominations: Committee and Floor Procedure*, by Elizabeth Rybicki.

Contents

Introduction.. 1

Senate Committee on Agriculture, Nutrition, and Forestry 5

Senate Committee on Armed Services.. 6

Senate Committee on Banking, Housing, and Urban Affairs 9

Senate Committee on the Budget... 12

Senate Committee on Commerce, Science, and Transportation 12

Senate Committee on Energy and Natural Resources 16

Senate Committee on Environment and Public Works... 18

Senate Committee on Finance 21

Senate Committee on Foreign Relations 24

Senate Committee on Health, Education, Labor, and Pensions.. 29

Senate Committee on Homeland Security and Governmental Affairs.. 33

Senate Committee on Indian Affairs.. 36

Senate Select Committee on Intelligence 37

Senate Committee on the Judiciary 38

Senate Committee on Rules and Administration 41

Senate Committee on Small Business and Entrepreneurship 41

Senate Committee on Veterans' Affairs 42

Tables

Table A-1. Positions That No Longer Require Senate Confirmation Per P.L. 112-166 43

Appendixes

Appendix. Presidential Appointee Positions That No Longer Require Senate
    Confirmation Per P.L. 112-166, the Presidential Appointment Efficiency and
    Streamlining Act of 2011 43

Contacts

Author Contact Information.. 45

Acknowledgment.. 45

Introduction

Under the Constitution, the President and the Senate share the power to appoint the principal officers of the United States. Almost all of the highest-level political appointee positions in the federal government are filled by these officers.[1] Three distinct stages mark the appointment process—selection and nomination by the President, consideration of the nomination by the Senate, and, if the nominee is confirmed, official appointment by the President.[2] During the confirmation process in the Senate, a nomination is first referred to one or more committees. If the committee or committees report the nomination to the full Senate, or are discharged from further consideration of the nomination, it is placed on the Senate's Executive Calendar and may be called up for floor consideration.[3] The following pages briefly describe the referral process and identify, for each committee to which referrals have been made, the positions that fall within the committee's jurisdiction.

Referral of Nominations to Senate Committees[4]

As part of the process of making an appointment to an advice and consent position, the President usually submits a nomination to the Senate. The Senate's executive clerk, acting on behalf of the Senate's presiding officer, refers the nomination to the appropriate committee or committees on the day it is received.[5] When making a referral, the executive clerk is guided by Senate Rule XXV, which establishes the subject matters under the purview of each committee and directs that "all proposed legislation, messages, petitions, memorials, and other matters relating primarily to [those] subjects" be referred to that committee. The executive clerk is also guided by precedents set by prior referrals and by standing orders and unanimous consent (UC) agreements pertaining to referral of nominations.

Most nominations are sent to a single committee. Occasionally, the Senate has agreed, by UC, standing order, or statute, to refer one or more nominations to more than one committee. Some UC agreements provided for such a multiple referral only in the case of a specific nomination, while other UC agreements applied to all future nominations to a particular position.

Nominations that are referred to more than one committee may be referred jointly or sequentially. If a nomination is referred jointly, the committees receive it simultaneously and may consider it concurrently. All committees to which a nomination is referred must report it to the full Senate or be discharged from its further consideration before it may be considered on the floor. In the case

---

[1] Positions in the White House Office to which the President makes appointments without the need for Senate confirmation are exceptions.

[2] In the final, official appointment stage, a confirmed nominee is given a commission signed by the President, with the seal of the United States affixed thereto, and is sworn into office.

[3] For more information on the Senate confirmation process, see CRS Report RL31980, *Senate Consideration of Presidential Nominations: Committee and Floor Procedure*, by Elizabeth Rybicki.

[4] For a general discussion of Senate committee referrals, see CRS Report 98-242, *Committee Jurisdiction and Referral in the Senate*, by Judy Schneider.

[5] As discussed below under the heading, "112th Congress Standing Order on Nominations," pursuant to a standing order adopted in the 112th Congress (2011-2012), certain specific nominations and categories of nominations are not referred to committee when received, but are subject to a potentially more expedited process of Senate consideration.

of a sequential referral, the nomination is referred first to the committee of predominant jurisdiction and referred sequentially to other committees as specified by the UC agreement or standing order. UC agreements for sequential referral can stipulate that the nomination must be reported out of the second committee within a specified period of time (usually 20 days), or else that committee will be automatically discharged from further consideration of the nomination.

Joint referral of a nomination has usually occurred when more than one committee appears to have had relatively equal jurisdictional claims. For example, since at least the beginning of the 109th Congress, nominations to eight positions—two each in the Department of Commerce and the Office of Management and Budget, and one each in the Department of Energy, Department of the Interior, Department of Labor, and Pension Benefit Guaranty Corporation—have been referred jointly to two committees.[6]

Sequential referral has been more likely when jurisdictional predominance appeared to favor one committee, but other committees also have had some jurisdictional claim on the nomination. In those instances, the nomination has usually been referred to the committee with predominant jurisdiction, and, after being reported to the full Senate by that committee, it has been referred sequentially to other committees. For example, since at least the beginning of the 109th Congress, the Senate has agreed, by UC, to refer sequentially nominations to most inspector general (IG) positions,[7] as well as four other positions—one in the Department of Defense, one in the Department of Justice, and two in the Department of Homeland Security.[8]

In a small number of cases, nominations have been referred to more than one committee on an ad hoc basis by UC. A 2004 nomination for Under Secretary of the Treasury for Enforcement,[9] for example, was first referred to the Committee on Finance. After the committee had reported the nomination, it was referred to the Committee on Banking, Housing, and Urban Affairs, and simultaneously re-referred to the Committee on Finance, pursuant to a UC agreement.[10] A 2006

---

[6] The positions are Under Secretary of Commerce for International Trade; Assistant Secretary of Commerce for Trade Promotion/Director General of the U.S. and Foreign Commercial Service; Director of the Office of Management and Budget; Deputy Director of the Office of Management and Budget; Assistant Secretary of Energy for Environmental Management; Assistant Secretary of the Interior for Fish, Wildlife, and Parks; Assistant Secretary of Labor for Veterans' Employment and Training Service; and Director of the Pension Benefit Guaranty Corporation.

[7] On January 9, 2007, the Senate agreed, by unanimous consent, "that nominations to the Office of Inspector General, except the Office of Inspector General of the Central Intelligence Agency, be referred in each case to the committee having primary jurisdiction over the department, agency or entity, and if and when reported in each case, then to the Committee on Homeland Security and Governmental Affairs for not to exceed 20 calendar days, except that in cases when the 20-day period expires while the Senate is in recess, the committee shall have an additional 5 calendar days after the Senate reconvenes to report the nomination and that if the nomination is not reported after the expiration of that period, the nomination be automatically discharged and placed on the executive calendar." Sen. Harry Reid, "Executive Nominations," remarks in the Senate, *Congressional Record*, vol. 153, part I, January 9, 2007, p. 487.

[8] These sequentially referred nominations include those to be the Assistant Secretary of the Army for Civil Works, which was referred to the Committee on Armed Services and the Committee on Environment and Public Works; the Assistant Attorney General for the National Security Division, which was referred to Committee on the Judiciary and the Select Committee on Intelligence; the Assistant Secretary of Homeland Security for U.S. Immigration and Customs Enforcement, which was referred, in two cases, to the Committee on Homeland Security and Governmental Affairs and the Committee on the Judiciary; and the Assistant Secretary of Homeland Security for the Transportation Security Administration, which was referred to the Committee on Commerce, Science, and Transportation and the Committee on Homeland Security and Governmental Affairs.

[9] This position is currently known in the Department of Treasury as Under Secretary for Terrorism and Financial Intelligence.

[10] Sen. Bill Frist, "Referral of Nominations," remarks in the Senate, *Congressional Record*, vol. 150, part 11, July 8, 2004, p. 14904.

---

nomination to be Assistant Secretary of State for Intelligence and Research was initially referred to the Committee on Foreign Relations. Two days after this referral, the committee was discharged from further consideration of the nomination, and the nomination was referred to the Select Committee on Intelligence, where it remains today, by UC.[11] Also in 2006, a nomination to the position of federal coordinator for Alaska Natural Gas Transportation Projects was initially referred to the Committee on Commerce, Science, and Transportation. Two weeks later, the Senate agreed, by UC, to discharge this committee from further consideration of the nomination, and to then refer the nomination to the Committee on Energy and Natural Resources,[12] where it remains today.

In some instances, different committees have exercised jurisdiction over different positions within the same department or agency. (For details, see the committee presentations that follow.) For example, six committees have jurisdiction over positions in the Department of Commerce, and four committees have jurisdiction over positions in the Department of the Interior. Usually, however, one committee has jurisdiction over most positions in a department or agency.

The appointment provisions for certain executive branch chief financial officers (CFOs) are unusual. The Chief Financial Officers Act of 1990, as amended, covers CFOs in 25 specified departments and agencies. Of these, 17 positions may be filled through appointment by the President, with the advice and consent of the Senate, or through designation by the President from among agency officials who have been confirmed by the Senate for other positions.[13] These CFO positions are identified under the appropriate committees in this report.

112th Congress Standing Order on Nominations

On June 29, 2011, the Senate adopted S.Res. 116, a resolution establishing special expedited procedures governing Senate consideration of certain presidential nominations.[14]

Under the terms of the resolution, which operates as a standing order of the Senate, 41 specified nominations or categories of nominations are, when received from the President, not referred to a Senate committee, but are instead placed directly on the Senate Executive Calendar under a newly created heading, "Privileged Nominations – Information Requested." A qualifying nomination will remain in this category until the Senate executive clerk receives written certification from the chairman of the committee with jurisdiction over the nomination that the "appropriate biographical and financial questionnaires have been received" from the nominee. Once certified in this way, the nomination in question is transferred by the executive clerk to a

---

[11] Sen. Mitch McConnell, "Referral of Discharged Nomination," remarks in the Senate, *Congressional Record*, vol. 152, part 8, June 14, 2006, p. 11186.

[12] Sen. Mitch McConnell, "Discharge and Referral," remarks in the Senate, *Congressional Record*, vol. 152, part 10, June 29, 2006, p. 13597.

[13] 31 U.S.C. §901(a)(1). For more information, see CRS Report RL31965, *Financial Management in the Federal Government: Efforts to Improve Performance*, by Virginia A. McMurtry; and CRS Report RL32550, *Homeland Security Financial Accountability Act: History and Recent Developments*, by Virginia A. McMurtry.

[14] In the 112th Congress, the Senate also passed legislation intended to reduce the number of executive branch positions subject to Senate confirmation. Enactment of S. 679 eliminates the requirement of Senate approval of several specified presidentially appointed positions in the federal agencies and departments. S. 679 passed the Senate on June 29, 2011, passed the House of Representatives on July 31, 2012, and was signed into law by the President on August 10, 2012, as P.L. 112-166. For additional information on these two measures, see CRS Report R41872, *Presidential Appointments, the Senate's Confirmation Process, and Changes Made in the 112th Congress*, by Maeve P. Carey.

separate section of the Executive Calendar having the heading, "Privileged Nomination – Information Received," and it will remain in this status on the calendar for 10 days of Senate session. At the expiration of this 10-day period, the nomination is placed on the "Nominations" section of the Executive Calendar, where nominations reported by Senate committees are listed. The sponsor of S.Res. 116 indicated his view that they would be placed in this position on the Executive Calendar, "with the presumption that these noncontroversial positions would be [confirmed] by unanimous consent."[15] Anytime that a nomination is on the Executive Calendar in either the "Information Requested" or "Information Received" section, any Senator, or on the behalf of another Senator, can direct that the nomination be referred to Senate committee in the usual fashion.

Organization of the Report

This report identifies, for each Senate committee to which nominations have been referred during recent Congresses, the positions over which the committee has exercised jurisdiction. The lists of presidentially appointed positions requiring Senate confirmation are based on referrals as of the date of passage of S. 679, which became P.L. 112-166 on August 10, 2012. A complete list of the presidentially appointed positions that no longer require Senate confirmation may be found in the **Appendix** at the end of this report. For each committee list, positions are categorized as full- or part-time and then grouped by department or agency. Where nominations have been referred to more than one committee, the organizations and titles are noted under each of the committees to which the nominations were referred. A footnote indicates the authority under which the referral to multiple committees was made.

Policy areas are not specified in statute for some of the sub-secretary positions. The policy areas shown in the listings for such positions are drawn from the text of presidential nomination messages and information from agency officials. In these cases, titles, specific responsibilities, and referral patterns may change over time.

Most appointments to departments and single-headed agencies are characterized by an indefinite tenure; office holders serve at the pleasure of the President. In contrast, terms of office for appointments to multi-member entities, such as commissions and boards, are often for fixed periods of time. For those positions that have fixed terms of office, the lists include the lengths of the terms.

Some commissions, councils, and other multi-member entities are required, by their enabling statutes, to maintain political balance in some way. This is noted in parentheses where applicable.

Nominations covered by S.Res. 116 are highlighted in the report with an asterisk, noting their privileged status under the standing order discussed above.

The information provided in this report was compiled from the Senate nominations database of the Legislative Information System,[16] which spans the 97th Congress to the present; data on departmental and agency websites; telephone conversations with agency officials; and the *United States Code*.

---

[15] Remarks of Sen. Charles E. Schumer, *Congressional Record*, daily edition, vol. 157 (June 29, 2011), p. S4203.

[16] The Legislative Information System, which is accessible to Congress, is available at http://www.congress.gov/nomis/ . A similar, publicly available database is at http://thomas.loc.gov/home/nomis.html.

Senate Committee on Agriculture, Nutrition, and Forestry

Full-Time Positions

Department of Agriculture[17]
Secretary
Deputy Secretary
Under Secretary—Farm and Foreign Agricultural Services
Under Secretary—Food, Nutrition, and Consumer Services
Under Secretary—Food Safety
Under Secretary—Marketing and Regulatory Programs
Under Secretary—Natural Resources and Environment
Under Secretary—Research, Education, and Economics
Under Secretary—Rural Development
Assistant Secretary—Civil Rights
*Assistant Secretary—Congressional Relations
*Chief Financial Officer[18]
General Counsel
Inspector General[19]

Commodity Futures Trading Commission (political balance required)
Commissioner—five positions (five-year terms of office—Chair must be confirmed as both a member and as chair.)

Farm Credit Administration (political balance required)
Member—three positions (six-year terms of office)

Part-Time Positions

Federal Agricultural Mortgage Corporation (Farmer Mac), Board of Directors
*Member—five (of 15 total) positions (indefinite terms of office; political balance required)

---

[17] For other positions within the department, see also Committee on Homeland Security and Governmental Affairs (for inspector general position).

[18] This chief financial officer (CFO) is one of the CFO positions covered by the Chief Financial Officers Act of 1990 (P.L. 101-576), as amended, that may be filled through appointment by the President, with the advice and consent of the Senate, or through designation by the President from among agency officials who have been confirmed by the Senate for other positions (31 U.S.C. §901(a)(1)).

[19] Pursuant to a UC agreement, most IG nominations are referred sequentially to the committee with predominant jurisdiction over the particular IG's agency and then the Committee on Homeland Security and Governmental Affairs. For more information, see footnote 7.

* Nomination covered by S.Res. 116 with privileged status under a standing order of the Senate. See "112th Congress Standing Order on Nominations" for further explanation.

Senate Committee on Armed Services

Full-Time Positions

Department of Defense[20]

Office of the Secretary
Secretary
Deputy Secretary
Under Secretary—Acquisition, Technology, and Logistics
Under Secretary—Comptroller/*Chief Financial Officer[21]
Under Secretary—Intelligence
Under Secretary—Personnel and Readiness
Under Secretary—Policy
Deputy Chief Management Officer
Principal Deputy Under Secretary—Acquisition, Technology, and Logistics
Principal Deputy Under Secretary—Comptroller
Principal Deputy Under Secretary—Intelligence
Principal Deputy Under Secretary—Personnel and Readiness
Principal Deputy Under Secretary—Policy
Assistant Secretary—Acquisition
Assistant Secretary—Asian and Pacific Security Affairs
Assistant Secretary—Global Strategic Affairs
Assistant Secretary—Health Affairs
Assistant Secretary—Homeland Defense and Americas' Security Affairs
Assistant Secretary—International Security Affairs
*Assistant Secretary—Legislative Affairs
Assistant Secretary—Logistics and Materiel Readiness
Assistant Secretary—Reserve Affairs
Assistant Secretary—Special Operations and Low-Intensity Conflict
Director—Cost Assessment and Program Evaluation
Director—Defense Research and Engineering
Director—Operational Energy Plans and Programs
Director—Operational Test and Evaluation
Assistant to the Secretary—Nuclear and Chemical and Biological Defense Programs
General Counsel
Inspector General[22]
Military Officers (commissions and promotions)

---

[20] See also Committee on Homeland Security and Governmental Affairs (for inspector general position).

[21] This chief financial officer (CFO) is one of the CFO positions covered by the Chief Financial Officers Act of 1990 (P.L. 101-576), as amended, that may be filled through appointment by the President, with the advice and consent of the Senate, or through designation by the President from among agency officials who have been confirmed by the Senate for other positions (31 U.S.C. §901(a)(1)).

* Nomination covered by S.Res. 116 with privileged status under a standing order of the Senate. See "112th Congress Standing Order on Nominations" for further explanation.

[22] Pursuant to a UC agreement, most IG nominations are referred sequentially to the committee with predominant jurisdiction over the particular IG's agency and then the Committee on Homeland Security and Governmental Affairs. (continued...)

Department of the Air Force
Secretary
Under Secretary
Assistant Secretary—Acquisition
*Assistant Secretary—Financial Management/Comptroller
Assistant Secretary—Manpower and Reserve Affairs
Assistant Secretary—Installations, Environment, and Logistics
General Counsel

Department of the Army
Secretary
Under Secretary
Assistant Secretary—Acquisition, Logistics, and Technology
Assistant Secretary—Civil Works[23]
*Assistant Secretary—Financial Management/Comptroller
Assistant Secretary—Installations and Environment
Assistant Secretary—Manpower and Reserve Affairs
General Counsel

Department of the Navy
Secretary
Under Secretary
*Assistant Secretary—Financial Management/Comptroller
Assistant Secretary—Energy, Installations, and Environment
Assistant Secretary—Manpower and Reserve Affairs
Assistant Secretary—Research, Development, and Acquisition
General Counsel

Joint Chiefs of Staff
Chairman (two-year term of office)
Vice Chairman (two-year term of office)
Chief of Staff (Air Force) (four-year term of office)
Chief of Staff (Army) (four-year term of office)
Chief of Naval Operations (four-year term of office)
Commandant of the Marine Corps (four-year term of office)

(...continued)

For more information, see footnote 7.

[23] As of October 31, 2007, the most recent nomination to this position had been referred sequentially to the Committee on Armed Services and the Committee on Environment and Public Works. On March 10, 2005, the Senate agreed, by unanimous consent, that "when the nomination for the Assistant Secretary for Civil Works is received by the Senate, it will be referred to the Committee on Armed Services; provided that when the Committee on Armed Services reports the nomination it be referred to the Committee on Environment and Public Works for a period of 20 days of session; provided further that if the Committee on Environment and Public Works does not report the nomination within those 20 days, the committee be discharged from further consideration of the nomination and the nomination be placed on the Calendar." Sen. Mitch McConnell, "Unanimous Consent Agreement—Executive Calendar," remarks in the Senate, *Congressional Record*, vol. 151, part 3, March 10, 2005, p. 4386.

* Nomination covered by S.Res. 116 with privileged status under a standing order of the Senate. See "112th Congress Standing Order on Nominations" for further explanation.

Department of Energy[24]
Under Secretary—Nuclear Security/Administrator—National Nuclear Security Administration (NNSA)
Principal Deputy Administrator—NNSA
Deputy Administrator—Defense Programs—NNSA
Deputy Administrator—Defense Nuclear Nonproliferation—NNSA
Assistant Secretary—Environmental Management[25]

Defense Nuclear Facilities Safety Board (political balance required)
Member—five positions (five-year terms of office)

U.S. Court of Appeals for the Armed Forces (political balance required)
Judge—five positions (15-year terms of office)

Part-Time Positions

Uniformed Services University of the Health Sciences, Board of Regents
Member—nine positions (six-year terms of office)

---

[24] For other positions within the department, see also Committee on Energy and Natural Resources and Committee on Homeland Security and Governmental Affairs (for inspector general position).

[25] Nominations to this position are referred jointly to the Committee on Armed Services and the Committee on Energy and Natural Resources pursuant to a standing order entered into by the Senate by unanimous consent on June 28, 1990. Sen. George Mitchell, "Joint Referral of Department of Energy Nomination," remarks in the Senate, *Congressional Record*, vol. 136, part 11, June 28, 1990, pp. 16573-16574.

Senate Committee on Banking, Housing, and Urban Affairs

Full-Time Positions

Department of Commerce[26]
Under Secretary—Export Administration[27]
Under Secretary—International Trade[28]
Assistant Secretary—Export Administration
Assistant Secretary—Export Enforcement
Assistant Secretary—Trade Promotion/Director General—U.S. and Foreign Commercial Service[29]

Department of Housing and Urban Development[30]
Secretary
Deputy Secretary
Assistant Secretary—Community Planning and Development
*Assistant Secretary—Congressional and Intergovernmental Relations
Assistant Secretary—Fair Housing and Equal Opportunity
Assistant Secretary—Housing/Federal Housing Commissioner
Assistant Secretary—Policy Development and Research
Assistant Secretary—Public and Indian Housing
*Chief Financial Officer[31]
Director—Office of Federal Housing Enterprise Oversight (five-year term)
General Counsel
Inspector General[32]
President—Government National Mortgage Association (Ginnie Mae)

---

[26] For other positions within the department, see also Committee on Commerce, Science, and Transportation; Committee on Environment and Public Works; Committee on Finance; Committee on Homeland Security and Governmental Affairs; and Committee on the Judiciary.

[27] Within the Department of Commerce, this position is also known as Under Secretary for Industry and Security.

[28] Nominations to this position are referred jointly to the Committee on Banking, Housing, and Urban Affairs and the Committee on Finance pursuant to a unanimous consent agreement of September 20, 2007. Sen. John Kerry, "Joint Referral," remarks in the Senate, *Congressional Record*, vol. 153, part 18, September 20, 2007, p. 25123.

[29] Nominations to this position are referred jointly to the Committee on Banking, Housing, and Urban Affairs and the Committee on Commerce, Science, and Transportation pursuant to a unanimous consent agreement of May 26, 2005. Sen. Bill Frist, "Joint Referral," remarks in the Senate, *Congressional Record*, vol. 151, part 8, May 26, 2005, p. 11590.

[30] See also Committee on Homeland Security and Governmental Affairs (for inspector general position).

[31] This chief financial officer (CFO) is one of CFO positions covered by the Chief Financial Officers Act of 1990 (P.L. 101-576), as amended, that may be filled through appointment by the President, with the advice and consent of the Senate, or through designation by the President from among agency officials who have been confirmed by the Senate for other positions (31 U.S.C. §901(a)(1)).

* Nomination covered by S.Res. 116 with privileged status under a standing order of the Senate. See "112th Congress Standing Order on Nominations" for further explanation.

[32] Pursuant to a UC agreement, most IG nominations are referred sequentially to the committee with predominant jurisdiction over the particular IG's agency and then the Committee on Homeland Security and Governmental Affairs. For more information, see footnote 7.

Department of Transportation[33]
Administrator—Federal Transit Administration

Department of the Treasury[34]
Under Secretary—Terrorism and Financial Crimes[35]
Assistant Secretary—Financial Institutions
Assistant Secretary—Financial Stability
Assistant Secretary—International Markets and Development
Assistant Secretary—Terrorist Financing
Special Inspector General for the Troubled Asset Relief Program[36]
Comptroller of the Currency (five-year term of office)
Director of the Mint (five-year term of office)
Director—Office of Financial Research (six-year term of office)
Director—Office of Thrift Supervision (five-year term of office)

Bureau of Consumer Financial Protection
Director

Council of Economic Advisers (Executive Office of the President)
Chair

Export-Import Bank[37] (political balance required)
Member—five positions (four-year terms of office—Chair must be confirmed as both a member and as chair.)
Inspector General[38]

---

[33] For other positions within the department, see also Committee on Commerce, Science, and Transportation; Committee on Environment and Public Works; and Committee on Homeland Security and Governmental Affairs (for inspector general position).

[34] For other positions within the department, see also Committee on Finance and Committee on Homeland Security and Governmental Affairs (for inspector general position).

[35] Nominations to this position are referred jointly to the Committee on Banking, Housing, and Urban Affairs and the Committee on Finance pursuant to a unanimous consent agreement of July 8, 2004. Sen. Bill Frist, "Referral of Nominations," remarks in the Senate, *Congressional Record*, vol. 150, part 11, July 8, 2004, p. 14904.

On April 8, 2004, Stuart Levey was nominated to be Under Secretary for Enforcement. The nomination was referred to the Committee on Finance, which reported it on May 20. Pursuant to a UC agreement of July 8, the nomination was referred to the Committee on Banking, Housing, and Urban Affairs, and simultaneously re-referred to the Committee on Finance (Sen. Bill Frist, "Referral of Nominations," remarks in the Senate, *Congressional Record*, vol. 150, part 11, July 8, 2004, p. 14904). The unanimous consent agreement stated that the agreement was to be specific to the nominations then at hand. The Committee on Banking, Housing, and Urban Affairs reported the nomination on July 20, and the Committee on Finance was discharged from further consideration pursuant to the July 8 agreement. The Senate confirmed the Levey nomination on July 21. The position of Under Secretary for Terrorism and Financial Crimes (or Under Secretary for Terrorism and Financial Intelligence, as it is known by the Department of the Treasury) was established by P.L. 108-447, Div. H, Title II, §222 (118 Stat. 3242) as a successor office to the Under Secretary for Enforcement, and Levey continued to serve in the new position until he announced his resignation on January 24, 2011.

[36] Established by the Economic Stabilization Act of 2008 (Section 121, P.L. 110-343; 12 USC 5231). Neil M. Barofsky was nominated November 17, 2008. As is the case with most inspectors general, Barofsky's nomination was sequentially referred to the Senate Homeland Security and Governmental Affairs Committee after it was reported out of the Senate Banking, Housing, and Urban Affairs Committee.

[37] See also Committee on Homeland Security and Governmental Affairs (for inspector general position).

[38] Pursuant to a UC agreement, most IG nominations are referred sequentially to the committee with predominant jurisdiction over the particular IG's agency and then the Committee on Homeland Security and Governmental Affairs. For more information, see footnote 7.

Federal Deposit Insurance Corporation[39] (political balance required)
Member—three positions (six-year terms of office—Chair and vice chair must be confirmed as both a member and as chair.)
Inspector General[40]

Federal Housing Finance Agency (political balance required)
Director[41]
Member—four positions (seven-year terms of office)
Inspector General[42]

Federal Reserve System, Board of Governors
Governor—seven positions (14-year terms of office—Chair and vice chair, who must be confirmed as both a governor and as chair and vice chair, also need to be confirmed for four-year terms in those offices.)

Financial Stability Oversight Council
Member—ten voting positions and five nonvoting (six-year terms of office)

National Credit Union Administration, Board of Directors (political balance required)
Member—three positions (six-year terms of office)

Securities and Exchange Commission (political balance required)
Commissioner—five positions (five-year terms of office)

Part-Time Positions

National Consumer Cooperative Bank, Board of Directors
*Member—three (of 15 total) positions (three-year terms of office)

National Institute of Building Sciences, Board of Directors
*Member—six (of 21 total) positions (three-year terms of office)

Securities Investor Protection Corporation, Board of Directors
*Director—five (of seven total) positions (three-year terms of office)[43]

---

[39] See also Committee on Homeland Security and Governmental Affairs (for inspector general position).

[40] Pursuant to a UC agreement, most IG nominations are referred sequentially to the committee with predominant jurisdiction over the particular IG's agency and then the Committee on Homeland Security and Governmental Affairs. For more information, see footnote 7.

[41] This position was established by the Housing and Economic Recovery Act of 2008 (P.L. 110-289; 122 Stat. 2654, Title I, Section 1101). Joseph A. Smith Jr. was nominated on November 15, 2010, and the nomination was returned to the President on December 22, 2010. To date there has been no additional nomination and the agency has an acting director.

[42] Pursuant to a UC agreement, most IG nominations are referred sequentially to the committee with predominant jurisdiction over the particular IG's agency and then the Committee on Homeland Security and Governmental Affairs.

For more information, see footnote 7.

* Nomination covered by S.Res. 116 with privileged status under a standing order of the Senate. See "112th Congress Standing Order on Nominations" for further explanation.

Senate Committee on the Budget

Full-Time Positions

Office of Management and Budget (Executive Office of the President)[44]
Director[45]
Deputy Director[46]

Senate Committee on Commerce, Science, and Transportation

Full-Time Positions

Department of Commerce[47]
Secretary
Deputy Secretary
Under Secretary—Economic Affairs
Under Secretary—Standards and Technology/ Director—National Institute of Standards and Technology
Assistant Secretary—*Administration/*Chief Financial Officer[48]
Assistant Secretary—Communications and Information
*Assistant Secretary—Legislative Affairs
Assistant Secretary—Manufacturing and Services
Assistant Secretary—Technology Policy
Assistant Secretary—Trade Promotion/Director General—U.S. and Foreign Commercial Service[49]

---

[44] For other positions within the Office of Management and Budget, see also Committee on Homeland Security and Governmental Affairs.

[45] On October 9, 2004, the Senate agreed to S.Res. 445 (108th Congress), which provided, in part, as follows: "The Committee on the Budget and the Committee on Homeland Security and Governmental Affairs shall have joint jurisdiction over the nominations of persons nominated by the President to fill the positions of Director and Deputy Director for Budget within the Office of Management and Budget, and if one committee votes to order reported such a nomination, the other must report within 30 calendar days session, or be automatically discharged" (§101(e)). Nominations to the positions of Director and Deputy Director of the Office of Management and Budget have been jointly referred to the two committees since the 109th Congress.

[46] Ibid. The Chief Financial Officer Act of 1990 designated the Deputy Director as the Deputy Director for Management and Finance and as the Chief Financial Officer of the U.S. (P.L. 101-576, Title II, Section 202(c)).

[47] For other positions within the department, see also Committee on Banking, Housing, and Urban Affairs; Committee on Environment and Public Works; Committee on Finance; Committee on Homeland Security and Governmental Affairs; and Committee on the Judiciary.

[48] This dual title position requires two separate nominations. Both nominations go to the Senate Committee on Commerce, Science, and Transportation. This chief financial officer (CFO) is one of the CFO positions covered by the Chief Financial Officers Act of 1990 (P.L. 101-576), as amended, that may be filled through appointment by the President, with the advice and consent of the Senate, or through designation by the President from among agency officials who have been confirmed by the Senate for other positions (31 U.S.C. §901(a)(1)).

[49] Nominations to this position are referred jointly to the Committee on Banking, Housing, and Urban Affairs and the (continued...)

General Counsel
Inspector General[50]

National Oceanic and Atmospheric Administration (NOAA)
Under Secretary—Oceans and Atmosphere/Administrator—NOAA
Assistant Secretary—Conservation and Management/Deputy Administrator—NOAA
Assistant Secretary—Environmental Observation and Prediction—NOAA

Department of Homeland Security[51]
Under Secretary—Science and Technology
Assistant Secretary/Administrator—Transportation Security Administration[52]
Commandant—United States Coast Guard
Officers (commissions and promotions)—United States Coast Guard Officers

Department of Transportation[53]
Secretary
Deputy Secretary
Under Secretary—Policy
Assistant Secretary—Aviation and International Affairs
*Assistant Secretary—Governmental Affairs
Assistant Secretary—Transportation Policy
Administrator—Federal Aviation Administration (five-year term of office)
Administrator—Federal Motor Carrier Safety Administration
Administrator—Federal Railroad Administration
Administrator—Maritime Administration
Administrator—National Highway Traffic Safety Administration
Administrator—Pipeline and Hazardous Materials Safety Administration
Administrator—Research and Innovative Technology Administration
*Chief Financial Officer[54]

(...continued)

Committee on Commerce, Science, and Transportation pursuant to a unanimous consent agreement of May 26, 2005. Sen. Bill Frist, "Joint Referral," remarks in the Senate, *Congressional Record*, vol. 151, part 8, May 26, 2005, p. 11590.

[50] Pursuant to a UC agreement, most IG nominations are referred sequentially to the committee with predominant jurisdiction over the particular IG's agency and then the Committee on Homeland Security and Governmental Affairs. For more information, see footnote 7.

* Nomination covered by S.Res. 116 with privileged status under a standing order of the Senate. See "112th Congress Standing Order on Nominations" for further explanation.

[51] For other positions within the department, see also Committee on Finance, Committee on Homeland Security and Governmental Affairs, and Committee on the Judiciary. The Homeland Security Act authorizes not more than 12 assistant secretaries to be appointed by the President with the advice and consent of the Senate (6 U.S.C. §113).

[52] Nominations to this position are referred sequentially to the Committee on Commerce, Science, and Transportation and the Committee on Homeland Security and Governmental Affairs.

[53] For other positions within the department, see also Committee on Banking, Housing, and Urban Affairs; Committee on Environment and Public Works; and Committee on Homeland Security and Governmental Affairs (for inspector general position).

[54] This chief financial officer (CFO) is one of the CFO positions covered by the Chief Financial Officers Act of 1990 (P.L. 101-576), as amended, that may be filled through appointment by the President, with the advice and consent of the Senate, or through designation by the President from among agency officials who have been confirmed by the Senate for other positions (31 U.S.C. §901(a)(1)).

General Counsel
Inspector General[55]

Consumer Product Safety Commission (political balance required)
Commissioner—five positions (seven-year terms of office—Only three of the positions have been funded and filled since the mid-1980s; the chair must be confirmed as both a member and the chair.)

Federal Communications Commission (political balance required)
Commissioner—five positions (five-year terms of office)

Federal Maritime Commission (political balance required)
Commissioner—five positions (five-year terms of office)

Federal Trade Commission (political balance required)
Commissioner—five positions (seven-year terms of office)

National Aeronautics and Space Administration[56]
Administrator
Deputy Administrator
*Chief Financial Officer
Inspector General[57]

National Transportation Safety Board (political balance required)
Member—five positions (five-year terms of office—the chair must be confirmed as both a member and as chair.)

Office of Science and Technology Policy (Executive Office of the President)
Director
Associate Director—Energy and Environment
Associate Director—National Security and International Affairs
Associate Director—Science
Associate Director—Technology/Chief Technology Officer

Surface Transportation Board (political balance required)
Member—three positions (five-year terms of office)

---

[55] Pursuant to a UC agreement, most IG nominations are referred sequentially to the committee with predominant jurisdiction over the particular IG's agency and then the Committee on Homeland Security and Governmental Affairs. For more information, see footnote 7.

* Nomination covered by S.Res. 116 with privileged status under a standing order of the Senate. See "112th Congress Standing Order on Nominations" for further explanation.

[56] See also Committee on Homeland Security and Governmental Affairs (for inspector general position).

[57] Pursuant to a UC agreement, most IG nominations are referred sequentially to the committee with predominant jurisdiction over the particular IG's agency and then the Committee on Homeland Security and Governmental Affairs. For more information, see footnote 7.

* Nomination covered by S.Res. 116 with privileged status under a standing order of the Senate. See "112th Congress Standing Order on Nominations" for further explanation.

Part-Time Positions

Corporation for Public Broadcasting Board of Directors (political balance required)
Member—nine positions (six-year terms of office)

Metropolitan Washington Airport Authority Board of Directors
*Member—three positions (six-year terms of office; political balance required)

AMTRAK, Board of Directors[58]
Member—seven positions (five-year terms of office)

Saint Lawrence Seaway Development Corporation Advisory Board (political balance required)
*Member—five positions (indefinite terms of office)

---

[58] Previously known as the AMTRAK Reform Board; name changed to AMTRAK Board of Directors with Title II, AMTRAK Reform and Operational Improvements, Section 202 of P.L. 110-432 (122 Stat. 4848), October 16, 2008.

* Nomination covered by S.Res. 116 with privileged status under a standing order of the Senate. See "112th Congress Standing Order on Nominations" for further explanation.

Senate Committee on Energy and Natural Resources

Full-Time Positions

Department of Energy[59]
Secretary
Deputy Secretary
Under Secretary
Under Secretary—Science
Administrator—Energy Information Administration
*Assistant Secretary—Congressional and Intergovernmental Affairs
Assistant Secretary—Electricity Delivery and Energy Reliability
Assistant Secretary—Energy Efficiency and Renewable Energy
Assistant Secretary—Environmental Management[60]
Assistant Secretary—Fossil Energy
Assistant Secretary—International Affairs and Domestic Policy
Assistant Secretary—Nuclear Energy
Director—Advanced Research Projects Agency-Energy
Director—Office of Civilian Radioactive Waste Management
Director—Office of Minority Economic Impact
Director—Office of Science
*Chief Financial Officer[61]
General Counsel
Inspector General[62]

---

[59] For other positions within the department, see also Committee on Armed Services and Committee on Homeland Security and Governmental Affairs (for inspector general position).

[60] Nominations to this position are referred jointly to the Committee on Armed Services and the Committee on Energy and Natural Resources pursuant to a standing order entered into by the Senate by unanimous consent on June 28, 1990. Sen. George Mitchell, "Joint Referral of Department of Energy Nomination," remarks in the Senate, *Congressional Record*, vol. 136, part 11, June 28, 1990, pp. 16573-16574.

[61] This chief financial officer (CFO) is one of the CFO positions covered by the Chief Financial Officers Act of 1990 (P.L. 101-576), as amended, that may be filled through appointment by the President, with the advice and consent of the Senate, or through designation by the President from among agency officials who have been confirmed by the Senate for other positions (31 U.S.C. §901(a)(1)).

[62] Pursuant to a UC agreement, most IG nominations are referred sequentially to the committee with predominant jurisdiction over the particular IG's agency and then the Committee on Homeland Security and Governmental Affairs. For more information, see footnote 7.

* Nomination covered by S.Res. 116 with privileged status under a standing order of the Senate. See "112th Congress Standing Order on Nominations" for further explanation.

Department of the Interior[63]
Secretary
Deputy Secretary
Assistant Secretary—Fish, Wildlife, and Parks[64]
Assistant Secretary—Insular Affairs
Assistant Secretary—Land and Minerals Management
*Assistant Secretary—Management, and Budget/Chief Financial Officer[65]
Assistant Secretary—Water and Science
Commissioner—Bureau of Reclamation
Director—Bureau of Land Management
Director—National Park Service
Director—Office of Surface Mining Reclamation and Enforcement
Director—U.S. Geological Survey
Inspector General[66]
Solicitor

Federal Energy Regulatory Commission (political balance required)
Commissioner—five positions (five-year terms of office)

Office of the Federal Coordinator for Alaska Natural Gas Transportation Projects
*Federal Coordinator[67]

---

[63] For other positions within the department, see also Committee on Environment and Public Works, Committee on Homeland Security and Governmental Affairs (for inspector general position), and Committee on Indian Affairs.

[64] Nominations to this position have been referred jointly to the Committee on Energy and Natural Resources and the Committee on Environment and Public Works pursuant to a unanimous consent agreement of April 26, 2007. Sen. Harry Reid, "Joint Referral of Nomination," remarks in the Senate, *Congressional Record*, daily edition, vol. 153, part 7, April 26, 2007, p. 10583.

[65] This chief financial officer (CFO) is one of the positions covered by the Chief Financial Officers Act of 1990 (P.L. 101-576), as amended, that may be filled through appointment by the President, with the advice and consent of the Senate, or through designation by the President from among agency officials who have been confirmed by the Senate for other positions (31 U.S.C. §901(a)(1)).

[66] Pursuant to a UC agreement, most IG nominations are referred sequentially to the committee with predominant jurisdiction over the particular IG's agency and then the Committee on Homeland Security and Governmental Affairs. For more information, see footnote 7.

[67] A June 12, 2006, nomination to this position was initially referred to the Committee on Commerce, Science, and Transportation. On June 29, 2006, the Senate agreed, by unanimous consent, that "the nomination of Drue Pearce to be the Federal Coordinator for Alaska Natural Gas Transportation Projects be discharged from the Committee on Commerce, Science, and Transportation and be referred to the Committee on Energy and Natural Resources." Sen. Mitch McConnell, "Discharge and Referral," remarks in the Senate, *Congressional Record*, vol. 152, part 10, June 29, 2006, p. 13597.

The term of the Federal Coordinator is "to last until 1 year following the completion of the project referred to in section 103" of the Alaska Natural Gas Pipeline Act (15 U.S.C. Section 720d(b)(1)). Section 103 discusses "an Alaska natural gas transportation project other than the Alaska natural gas transportation system" (15 U.S.C. 720a(a)).

* Nomination covered by S.Res. 116 with privileged status under a standing order of the Senate. See "112th Congress Standing Order on Nominations" for further explanation.

Senate Committee on Environment and Public Works

Full-Time Positions

Department of Commerce[68]
Assistant Secretary—Economic Development

Department of Defense[69]
Assistant Secretary—Army—Civil Works[70]

Department of the Interior[71]
Assistant Secretary—Fish, Wildlife and Parks[72]
Director—U.S. Fish and Wildlife Service

Department of Transportation[73]
Administrator—Federal Highway Administration

Appalachian Regional Commission
Federal Cochair

Chemical Safety and Hazard Investigation Board
Member—five positions (five-year terms of office—the chair must be confirmed as both a member and as chair.)

---

[68] For other positions within the department, see also Committee on Banking, Housing, and Urban Affairs; Committee on Commerce, Science, and Transportation; Committee on Finance; Committee on Homeland Security and Governmental Affairs; and Committee on the Judiciary.

[69] For other positions within the department, see also Committee on Armed Services and Committee on Homeland Security and Governmental Affairs (for inspector general position).

[70] Nominations to this position are referred sequentially to the Committee on Armed Services and the Committee on Environment and Public Works. On March 10, 2005, the Senate agreed, by unanimous consent, that "when the nomination for the Assistant Secretary for Civil Works is received by the Senate, it be referred to the Committee on Armed Services; provided that when the Committee on Armed Services reports the nomination it be referred to the Committee on Environment and Public Works for a period of 20 days of session; provided further that if the Committee on Environment and Public Works does not report the nomination within those 20 days, the committee be discharged from further consideration of the nomination and the nomination be placed on the Calendar." Sen. Mitch McConnell, "Unanimous Consent Agreement—Executive Calendar," remarks in the Senate, *Congressional Record*, vol. 151, part 3, March 10, 2005, p. 4386.

[71] For other positions within the department, see also Committee on Energy and Natural Resources, Committee on Homeland Security and Governmental Affairs (for inspector general position), and Committee on Indian Affairs.

[72] Nominations to this position are referred jointly to the Committee on Energy and Natural Resources and the Committee on Environment and Public Works pursuant to a unanimous consent agreement of April 26, 2007. Sen. Harry Reid, "Joint Referral of Nomination," remarks in the Senate, *Congressional Record*, vol. 153, part 7, April 26, 2007, p. 10583.

[73] For other positions within the department, see also Committee on Banking, Housing, and Urban Affairs; Committee on Homeland Security and Governmental Affairs (for inspector general position); and Committee on Commerce, Science, and Transportation.

Council on Environmental Quality (Executive Office of the President)[74]
Chair

Delta Regional Authority
Federal Cochair

Environmental Protection Agency[75]
Administrator
Deputy Administrator
Assistant Administrator—Administration and Resources Management
Assistant Administrator—Air and Radiation
Assistant Administrator—Enforcement and Compliance Assurance
Assistant Administrator—Environmental Information/Chief Information Officer
Assistant Administrator—International and Tribal Affairs
Assistant Administrator—Prevention, Pesticides, and Toxic Substances
Assistant Administrator—Research and Development
Assistant Administrator—Solid Waste and Emergency Response
Assistant Administrator—Toxic Substances[76]
Assistant Administrator—Water
*Chief Financial Officer[77]
General Counsel
Inspector General[78]

Northern Border Regional Commission
Federal Cochair

Nuclear Regulatory Commission[79] (political balance required)
Commissioner—five positions (five-year terms of office)
Inspector General[80]

---

[74] Chair is confirmed as a member and designated as chair by the President (42 USC §4342). Composition of Council on Environmental Quality: Act August 2, 2005, P.L. 109-54, Title III, 119 Stat. 543, provides: "Notwithstanding section 202 of the National Environmental Policy Act of 1970 [this section], the Council [on Environmental Quality] shall consist of one member, appointed by the President, by and with the advice and consent of the Senate, serving as chairman and exercising all powers, functions, and duties of the Council."

[75] See also Committee on Homeland Security and Governmental Affairs (for inspector general position).

[76] In the EPA this position is considered to be the assistant administrator for the Office of Chemical Safety and Pollution Prevention (OCSPP); title as nominated is not used per telephone verification with the OCSPP on 1/25/2012.

[77] This chief financial officer (CFO) is one of the CFO positions covered by the Chief Financial Officers Act of 1990 (P.L. 101-576), as amended, that may be filled through appointment by the President, with the advice and consent of the Senate, or through designation by the President from among agency officials who have been confirmed by the Senate for other positions (31 U.S.C. §901(a)(1)).

* Nomination covered by S.Res. 116 with privileged status under a standing order of the Senate. See "112th Congress Standing Order on Nominations" for further explanation.

[78] Pursuant to a UC agreement, most IG nominations are referred sequentially to the committee with predominant jurisdiction over the particular IG's agency and then the Committee on Homeland Security and Governmental Affairs. For more information, see footnote 7.

[79] See also Committee on Homeland Security and Governmental Affairs (for inspector general position).

[80] Pursuant to a UC agreement, most IG nominations are referred sequentially to the committee with predominant jurisdiction over the particular IG's agency and then the Committee on Homeland Security and Governmental Affairs. For more information, see footnote 7.

Office of Environmental Quality
Deputy Director[81]

Part-Time Positions

Morris K. Udall Scholarship and Excellence in National Environmental Policy Foundation, Board of Trustees (political balance required)
*Member—nine positions (six-year terms of office)

Tennessee Valley Authority, Board of Directors[82]
Member—nine positions (five-year terms of office)
Inspector General[83]

---

[81] There is established in the Executive Office of the President an office to be known as the Office of Environmental Quality (hereinafter in this title [42 USCS §§4371 et seq.] referred to as the "Office"). The Chairman of the Council on Environmental Quality established by Public Law 91-190 [42 USCS §§4321 et seq.] shall be the Director of the Office. There shall be in the Office a Deputy Director who shall be appointed by the President, by and with the advice and consent of the Senate.

(b) Compensation of Deputy Director. The compensation of the Deputy Director shall be fixed by the President at a rate not in excess of the annual rate of compensation payable to the Deputy Director of the Bureau of the Budget [Deputy Director of the Office of Management and Budget].

[82] See also Committee on Homeland Security and Governmental Affairs (for inspector general position).

[83] Pursuant to a UC agreement, most IG nominations are referred sequentially to the committee with predominant jurisdiction over the particular IG's agency and then the Committee on Homeland Security and Governmental Affairs. For more information, see footnote 7.

* Nomination covered by S.Res. 116 with privileged status under a standing order of the Senate. See "112th Congress Standing Order on Nominations" for further explanation.

Senate Committee on Finance

Full-Time Positions

Department of Commerce[84]
Under Secretary—International Trade[85]
Assistant Secretary—Import Administration
Assistant Secretary—Market Access and Compliance

Department of Health and Human Services[86]
Secretary
Deputy Secretary
Administrator—Centers for Medicare and Medicaid Services
*Assistant Secretary—Resources and Technology[87]/Chief Financial Officer[88]
Assistant Secretary—Family Support
Assistant Secretary—Legislation
Assistant Secretary—Planning and Evaluation
Assistant Secretary—Public Affairs
Commissioner—Children, Youth, and Families
General Counsel
Inspector General[89]

Department of Homeland Security[90]
Commissioner—U.S. Customs and Border Protection

---

[84] For other positions within the department, see also Committee on Banking, Housing, and Urban Affairs; Committee on Commerce, Science, and Transportation; Committee on Environment and Public Works; Committee on Homeland Security and Governmental Affairs; and Committee on the Judiciary.

[85] As of December 22, 2010, the most recent nomination to this position had been referred jointly to the Committee on Banking, Housing, and Urban Affairs and the Committee on Finance pursuant to a unanimous consent agreement of September 29, 2005. Sen. Bill Frist, "Joint Referral of Nomination," remarks in the Senate, *Congressional Record*, vol. 151, part 16, September 29, 2005, p. 21774.

[86] For other positions within the department, see also Committee on Homeland Security and Governmental Affairs (for inspector general position); Committee on Health, Education, Labor, and Pensions; and Committee on Indian Affairs.

[87] Within the Department of Health and Human Services, this position is known as Assistant Secretary for Financial Resources and Chief Financial Officer.

[88] This chief financial officer (CFO) is one of the CFO positions covered by the Chief Financial Officers Act of 1990 (P.L. 101-576), as amended, that may be filled through appointment by the President, with the advice and consent of the Senate, or through designation by the President from among agency officials who have been confirmed by the Senate for other positions (31 U.S.C. §901(a)(1)).

[89] Pursuant to a UC agreement, most IG nominations are referred sequentially to the committee with predominant jurisdiction over the particular IG's agency and then the Committee on Homeland Security and Governmental Affairs. For more information, see footnote 7.

* Nomination covered by S.Res. 116 with privileged status under a standing order of the Senate. See "112th Congress Standing Order on Nominations" for further explanation.

[90] For other positions within the department, see also Committee on Commerce, Science, and Transportation; Committee on Homeland Security and Governmental Affairs; and Committee on the Judiciary. The Homeland Security Act authorizes not more than 12 assistant secretaries to be appointed by the President with the advice and consent of the Senate (6 U.S.C. §113). As of April 15, 2011 eleven assistant secretaries had been nominated and confirmed.

Department of the Treasury[91]
Secretary
Deputy Secretary
Under Secretary—Domestic Finance
Under Secretary—International Affairs
Under Secretary—Terrorism and Financial Crimes[92]
Assistant Secretary—Economic Policy
Assistant Secretary—Financial Markets
Assistant Secretary (Deputy Under Secretary)—International Affairs[93]
Assistant Secretary—Tax Policy
*Assistant Secretary (Deputy Under Secretary)—Legislative Affairs[94]
*Chief Financial Officer[95]
Chief Counsel—Internal Revenue Service/Assistant General Counsel for Tax
Commissioner—Internal Revenue (five-year terms of office)
General Counsel
Inspector General[96]
Inspector General—Tax Administration[97]

Office of United States Trade Representative (Executive Office of the President)
U.S. Trade Representative
Deputy U.S. Trade Representative
Deputy U.S. Trade Representative

---

[91] For other positions within the department, see also Committee on Banking, Housing, and Urban Affairs and Committee on Homeland Security and Governmental Affairs (for inspector general position).

[92] On April 8, 2004, Stuart Levey was nominated to be Under Secretary for Enforcement. The nomination was referred to the Committee on Finance, which reported it on May 20. Pursuant to a UC agreement of July 8, the nomination was referred to the Committee on Banking, Housing, and Urban Affairs, and simultaneously re-referred to the Committee on Finance (Sen. Bill Frist, "Referral of Nominations," remarks in the Senate, *Congressional Record*, vol. 150, part 11, July 8, 2004, p. 14904`). The UC agreement stated that the agreement was to be specific to the nominations then at hand. The Committee on Banking, Housing, and Urban Affairs reported the nomination on July 20, and the Committee on Finance was discharged from further consideration pursuant to the July 8 agreement. The Senate confirmed the Levey nomination on July 21. The position of Under Secretary for Terrorism and Financial Crimes (or Under Secretary for Terrorism and Financial Intelligence, as it is known by the Department of the Treasury) was established by P.L. 108-447, Div. H, Title II, §222 (118 Stat. 3242) as a successor office to the Under Secretary for Enforcement, and Levey continued to serve in the new position until he announced his resignation on January 24, 2011.

[93] Under the provisions of 31 U.S.C. §301(d), the Department of the Treasury has two deputy under secretaries who are to be appointed by the President, with the advice and consent of the Senate. Section 301(d) also provides the "[w]hen appointing each Deputy Under Secretary, the President may designate the Deputy Under Secretary as an Assistant Secretary." As of April 15, 2011, the most recent appointees to Deputy Under Secretary for International Affairs and Deputy Under Secretary for Legislative Affairs were identified as assistant secretaries on the Department of Treasury website at http://www.ustreas.gov/.

[94] Ibid.

[95] This chief financial officer (CFO) is one of the CFO positions covered by the Chief Financial Officers Act of 1990 (P.L. 101-576), as amended, that may be filled through appointment by the President, with the advice and consent of the Senate, or through designation by the President from among agency officials who have been confirmed by the Senate for other positions (31 U.S.C. §901(a)(1)).

* Nomination covered by S.Res. 116 with privileged status under a standing order of the Senate. See "112th Congress Standing Order on Nominations" for further explanation.

[96] Pursuant to a UC agreement, most IG nominations are referred sequentially to the committee with predominant jurisdiction over the particular IG's agency and then the Committee on Homeland Security and Governmental Affairs. For more information, see footnote 7.

[97] Ibid.

Deputy U.S. Trade Representative
Chief Agricultural Negotiator

Pension Benefit Guaranty Corporation
Director[98]

Social Security Administration[99]
Commissioner (six-year term of office)
Deputy Commissioner (six-year term of office)
Inspector General[100]

United States International Trade Commission (political balance required)
Commissioner—six positions (nine-year terms of office)

United States Tax Court
Judge—19 positions (15-year terms of office)

Part-Time Positions

Federal Hospital Insurance Trust Fund, Board of Trustees (political balance required)
*Member—two (of six total) positions (four-year terms of office)

Federal Old-Age and Survivors Trust Fund and the Disability Insurance Trust Fund, Board of Trustees (political balance required)
*Member—two (of six total) positions (four-year terms of office)

***Federal Supplementary Medical Insurance Trust Fund, Board of Trustees** (political balance required)
Member—two (of six total) positions (four-year terms of office)

Internal Revenue Service Oversight Board
*Member—seven (of nine total) positions (five-year terms of office)

Social Security Advisory Board (political balance required)
*Member—three (of seven total) positions (six-year terms of office)[101]

---

[98] The Director of the Pension Benefit Guaranty Corporation was established as a position to which appointments are made by the President, with the advice and consent of the Senate, by the Pension Protection Act of 2006 (P.L. 109-280, §411; 120 Stat. 935). The act provides that "[t]he Committee on Finance of the Senate and the Committee on Health, Education, Labor, and Pensions of the Senate shall have joint jurisdiction over the nomination of a person nominated by the President to fill [this position], and if one committee votes to order reported such a nomination, the other shall report within 30 calendar days, or be automatically discharged" (P.L. 109-280, §411(c)(1); 120 Stat. 935). The act also provides that the executive director at the time of enactment, "or any other individual, may serve as interim Director ... until an individual is appointed as Director" under the advice and consent process (P.L. 109-280, §411(d); 120 Stat. 936). The first nomination to this position was received by the Senate on May 3, 2007, and was referred as specified in the law to the Senate Committees on Finance; and Health, Education, Labor, and Pensions.

[99] See also Committee on Homeland Security and Governmental Affairs (for inspector general position).

[100] Pursuant to a UC agreement, most IG nominations are referred sequentially to the committee with predominant jurisdiction over the particular IG's agency and then the Committee on Homeland Security and Governmental Affairs. For more information, see footnote 7.

* Nomination covered by S.Res. 116 with privileged status under a standing order of the Senate. See "112th Congress (continued...)

Senate Committee on Foreign Relations

Full-Time Positions

Department of State[102]
Secretary
Deputy Secretary
Deputy Secretary—Management and Resources
Under Secretary—Arms Control and International Security
Under Secretary—Economic, Energy and Agricultural Affairs
Under Secretary—Civilian Security, Democracy, and Human Rights
Under Secretary—Management
Under Secretary—Political Affairs
Under Secretary—Public Diplomacy and Public Affairs
Assistant Secretary—African Affairs[103]
Assistant Secretary—Arms Control, Verification and Compliance
Assistant Secretary—Budget and Planning/*Chief Financial Officer[104]
Assistant Secretary—Conflict and Stabilization Operations
Assistant Secretary—Consular Affairs
Assistant Secretary—Democracy, Human Rights and Labor
Assistant Secretary—Diplomatic Security/Director—Office of Foreign Missions[105]
Assistant Secretary—East Asian and Pacific Affairs
Assistant Secretary—Economic, Energy and Business Affairs
Assistant Secretary—Educational and Cultural Affairs
Assistant Secretary—European and Eurasian Affairs
Assistant Secretary—International Narcotics and Law Enforcement Affairs
Assistant Secretary—International Organization Affairs
Assistant Secretary—International Security and Nonproliferation
*Assistant Secretary—Legislative Affairs
Assistant Secretary—Near Eastern Affairs
Assistant Secretary—Oceans and International Environmental and Scientific Affairs

---

(...continued)

Standing Order on Nominations" for further explanation.

[102] For other positions within the department, see also Committee on Homeland Security and Governmental Affairs (for inspector general position), and Select Committee on Intelligence.

[103] Although not guaranteed, the two most recent Assistant Secretaries—African Affairs also held the advice and consent part-time position as a member of the Board of Directors of the African Development Foundation.

[104] The chief financial officer (CFO) may be appointed by the President, with the advice and consent of the Senate, or may be designated by the President from among agency officials who have been confirmed by the Senate for other positions (31 U.S.C. §901(a)(1)). With regard to State Department appointments, since 2001 through the 110th Congress, the same individual had been separately and simultaneously nominated for, and confirmed to, the positions of CFO and Assistant Secretary for Resource Management. In 2011, this office was renamed the Bureau of Budget and Planning.

[105] Nomination must be made and confirmed for both positions.

* Nomination covered by S.Res. 116 with privileged status under a standing order of the Senate. See "112th Congress Standing Order on Nominations" for further explanation.

Assistant Secretary—Political-Military Affairs
Assistant Secretary—Population, Refugees and Migration
Assistant Secretary—South and Central Asian Affairs
Assistant Secretary—Western Hemisphere Affairs
Ambassador-at-Large—Coordinator—Counterterrorism
Ambassador-at-Large—Global Women's Issues
Ambassador-at-Large—Director—Office to Monitor and Combat Trafficking in Persons
Ambassador-at-Large—International Religious Freedom
Ambassador-at-Large—War Crimes Issues
U.S. Permanent Representative to the Organization of American States
U.S. Permanent Representative to the North Atlantic Treaty Organization
Coordinator—Reconstruction and Stabilization
Coordinator—U.S. Global AIDS
Director General—Foreign Service
*Chief Financial Officer[106]
Inspector General[107]
Legal Adviser
Chief of Protocol[108]
Ambassadors

Foreign Service Officers (numerous commissions and promotions)

U.S. Mission to the United Nations
U.S. Permanent Representative and Chief of Mission—United Nations
U.S. Deputy Permanent Representative—United Nations
U.S. Representative—United Nations Economic and Social Council
U.S. Alternate Representative—Special Political Affairs in the United Nations
U.S. Representative—United Nations Management and Reform
U.S. Representative—European Office of the United Nations (Geneva)
U.S. Representative—Vienna Office of the United Nations (also serves as a representative to the International Atomic Energy Agency)
U.S. Representative—International Atomic Energy Agency
U.S. Deputy Representative—International Atomic Energy Agency
U.S. Representative and Alternate Representatives to sessions of the General Assembly and other United Nations Bodies—numerous positions (terms of office depends on length of session)

---

[106] This chief financial officer (CFO) is one of the CFO positions covered by the Chief Financial Officers Act of 1990 (P.L. 101-576), as amended, that may be filled through appointment by the President, with the advice and consent of the Senate, or through designation by the President from among agency officials who have been confirmed by the Senate for other positions (31 U.S.C. §901(a)(1)).

[107] Pursuant to a UC agreement, most IG nominations are referred sequentially to the committee with predominant jurisdiction over the particular IG's agency and then the Committee on Homeland Security and Governmental Affairs. For more information, see footnote 7.

[108] According to the State Department, "Since 1961, the Chief of Protocol has been commissioned an Ambassador, requiring the President's nominee to be confirmed by the Senate." Quote from the State Department website, available at http://www.state.gov/s/cpr/c15634.htm.

* Nomination covered by S.Res. 116 with privileged status under a standing order of the Senate. See "112th Congress Standing Order on Nominations" for further explanation.

U.S. Agency for International Development[109]
Administrator
Deputy Administrator
Assistant Administrator—Sub-Saharan Africa
Assistant Administrator—Asia
Assistant Administrator—Europe and Eurasia
Assistant Administrator—Food Safety
Assistant Administrator—Global Health
Assistant Administrator—Democracy, Conflict, and Humanitarian Assistance
Assistant Administrator—Latin America and Caribbean
Assistant Administrator—Middle East
*Assistant Administrator—Legislative and Public Affairs
Assistant Administrator—Policy, Planning and Learning
Assistant Administrator—Economic Growth, Agriculture, and Trade
Inspector General[110]

European Bank for Reconstruction and Development
U.S. Executive Director

International Broadcasting Bureau, Broadcasting Board of Governors
Director

International Joint Commission, United States and Canada
Commissioner—three positions

International Monetary Fund
U.S. Executive Director (two-year term of office)
U.S. Alternate Executive Director (two-year term of office)

Inter-American Development Bank
U.S. Executive Director (three-year term of office—The incumbent of this position also serves as U.S. Executive Director for the Inter-American Investment Corporation.)

U.S. Alternate Executive Director (three-year term of office—The incumbent of this position also serves as U.S. Alternate Executive Director for the Inter-American Investment Corporation.)

U.S. Trade and Development Agency
Director

---

[109] See also Committee on Homeland Security and Governmental Affairs (for inspector general position).

[110] Pursuant to a UC agreement, most IG nominations are referred sequentially to the committee with predominant jurisdiction over the particular IG's agency and then the Committee on Homeland Security and Governmental Affairs. For more information, see footnote 7.

* Nomination covered by S.Res. 116 with privileged status under a standing order of the Senate. See "112th Congress Standing Order on Nominations" for further explanation.

Organizations with Full- and Part-Time Positions[111]

African Development Bank
U.S. Executive Director (five-year term of office; full-time)
Governor and Alternate Governor (five-year terms of office; part-time)

Asian Development Bank
U.S. Executive Director (full-time)
Governor and Alternate Governor (part-time)

International Bank for Reconstruction and Development
U.S. Executive Director (two-year term of office; full-time—The incumbent also serves as U.S. Executive Director for the International Finance Corporation and the International Development Association.)

U.S. Alternate Executive Director (two-year term of office; full-time—The incumbent also serves as U.S. Alternate Executive Director for the International Finance Corporation and the International Development Association.)

Governor (same individual as the International Monetary Fund Governor; five-year term of office; part-time—The incumbent also serves as Governor for the International Finance Corporation and the International Development Association.)

Alternate Governor (five-year term of office; part-time—The incumbent also serves as Alternate Governor for the International Finance Corporation and the International Development Association.)

Millennium Challenge Corporation
Chief Executive Officer (full-time)
*Member, Board of Directors—four (of nine total) positions (part-time; three-year terms of office)

Overseas Private Investment Corporation
President/Chief Executive Officer (full-time)
Executive Vice President (full-time)
*Member, Board of Directors—eight (of 15 total) positions (part-time; three-year terms of office)

Peace Corps
Director (full-time)
Deputy Director (full-time)
*Member, National Peace Corps Advisory Council—15 positions (part-time; political balance required; two-year terms of office)

---

[111] Because several organizations under this committee have both full- and part-time advice and consent positions, they were listed under this heading for succinctness.

* Nomination covered by S.Res. 116 with privileged status under a standing order of the Senate. See "112th Congress Standing Order on Nominations" for further explanation.

Part-Time Positions

Advisory Board for Cuba Broadcasting (political balance required)[112]
*Member—eight positions (three-year terms of office)

African Development Foundation, Board of Directors (political balance required)
*Member—seven positions (six-year terms of office)[113]

African Development Fund
Governor and Alternate Governor

Broadcasting Board of Governors (political balance required)
Member—eight (of nine total) positions (three-year terms of office)

Inter-American Foundation, Board of Directors (political balance required)
*Member—nine positions (six-year terms of office)

U.S. Advisory Commission on Public Diplomacy[114] (political balance required)
*Commissioner—seven positions (three-year terms of office)

---

[112] The Office of the Assistant to the President for Legislative Affairs at the White House has confirmed that there has not been a nomination to the Board since a nomination in January 2005 that was subsequently confirmed by the Senate in June 2005.

[113] Although not guaranteed, the two most recent Assistant Secretaries—African Affairs also held the advice and consent part-time position as a member of the Board of Directors of the African Development Foundation.

[114] Nominations to these positions are processed by the State Department. (Communication with State Department official, July 2, 2007.)

* Nomination covered by S.Res. 116 with privileged status under a standing order of the Senate. See "112th Congress Standing Order on Nominations" for further explanation.

Senate Committee on Health, Education, Labor, and Pensions

Full-Time Positions

Department of Education[115]
Secretary
Deputy Secretary
Under Secretary
Assistant Secretary—Civil Rights
Assistant Secretary—Communications and Outreach
Assistant Secretary—Elementary and Secondary Education
*Assistant Secretary—Legislation and Congressional Affairs
Assistant Secretary—Planning, Evaluation and Policy Development
Assistant Secretary—Postsecondary Education
Assistant Secretary—Special Education and Rehabilitative Services
Assistant Secretary—Vocational and Adult Education
*Chief Financial Officer[116]
*Commissioner—Rehabilitation Services Administration
Director—Institute of Education Sciences (six-year term of office)
General Counsel
Inspector General[117]

Department of Health and Human Services[118]
Administrator—Substance Abuse and Mental Health Services Administration
Assistant Secretary—Aging
Assistant Secretary—Health
*Assistant Secretary—Legislation
Assistant Secretary—Preparedness and Response
*Commissioner—Administration for Children, Youth, Families
Commissioner—Food and Drugs
Director—National Institutes of Health
Surgeon General (four-year term of office)
Public Health Service—Officer Corps

---

[115] See also Committee on Homeland Security and Governmental Affairs (for inspector general position).

[116] This chief financial officer (CFO) is one of the positions covered by the Chief Financial Officers Act of 1990 (P.L. 101-576), as amended, that may be filled through appointment by the President, with the advice and consent of the Senate, or through designation by the President from among agency officials who have been confirmed by the Senate for other positions (31 U.S.C. §901(a)(1)).

[117] Pursuant to a UC agreement, most IG nominations are referred sequentially to the committee with predominant jurisdiction over the particular IG's agency and then the Committee on Homeland Security and Governmental Affairs. For more information, see footnote 7.

[118] For other positions within the department, see also Committee on Finance, Committee on Homeland Security and Governmental Affairs (for inspector general position), and Committee on Indian Affairs.

* Nomination covered by S.Res. 116 with privileged status under a standing order of the Senate. See "112th Congress Standing Order on Nominations" for further explanation.

Department of Labor[119]
Secretary
Deputy Secretary
*Assistant Secretary—Congressional and Intergovernmental Affairs
Assistant Secretary—Disability Employment Policy
Assistant Secretary—Employee Benefits Security Administration
Assistant Secretary—Employment and Training Administration
Assistant Secretary—Mine Safety and Health Administration
Assistant Secretary—Occupational Safety and Health Administration
Assistant Secretary—Policy
Assistant Secretary—Veterans' Employment and Training Service[120]
Administrator—Wage and Hour Division
Commissioner—Bureau of Labor Statistics
*Chief Financial Officer[121]
Inspector General[122]
Solicitor

Corporation for National and Community Service[123]
Chief Executive Officer
Inspector General[124]

Equal Employment Opportunity Commission (political balance required)
Commissioner—five positions (five-year terms of office)
General Counsel (four-year term of office)

Federal Mediation and Conciliation Service
Director

Federal Mine Safety and Health Review Commission
Commissioner—five positions (six-year terms of office)

---

[119] For other positions within the department, see also Committee on Homeland Security and Governmental Affairs (for inspector general position) and Committee on Veterans' Affairs.

[120] Nominations to this position are jointly referred to the Committee on Health, Education, Labor, and Pensions and the Committee on Veterans' Affairs pursuant to a unanimous consent agreement of May 24, 2005. Sen. Bill Frist, "Joint Referral," remarks in the Senate, *Congressional Record*, vol. 151, part 8, May 24, 2005, p. 10958.

[121] This chief financial officer (CFO) is one of the CFO positions covered by the Chief Financial Officers Act of 1990 (P.L. 101-576), as amended, that may be filled through appointment by the President, with the advice and consent of the Senate, or through designation by the President from among agency officials who have been confirmed by the Senate for other positions (31 U.S.C. §901(a)(1)).

[122] Pursuant to a UC agreement, most IG nominations are referred sequentially to the committee with predominant jurisdiction over the particular IG's agency and then the Committee on Homeland Security and Governmental Affairs. For more information, see footnote 7.

* Nomination covered by S.Res. 116 with privileged status under a standing order of the Senate. See "112th Congress Standing Order on Nominations" for further explanation.

[123] See also Committee on Homeland Security and Governmental Affairs (for inspector general position).

[124] Pursuant to a UC agreement, most IG nominations are referred sequentially to the committee with predominant jurisdiction over the particular IG's agency and then the Committee on Homeland Security and Governmental Affairs. For more information, see footnote 7.

National Foundation on the Arts and the Humanities
National Endowment for the Arts—Chair (four-year term of office)
National Endowment for the Humanities—Chair (four-year term of office)
Institute of Museum and Library Services—Director (four-year term of office)

National Labor Relations Board (Political balance is not required, but, by tradition, no more than three members are from the same party.)
Member—five positions (five-year terms of office)
General Counsel (four-year term of office)

National Mediation Board (political balance required)
Member—three positions (three-year terms of office)

National Science Board
Member—twenty-four positions (six-year terms of office)

National Science Foundation
Director (six-year term of office)
Deputy Director

Occupational Safety and Health Review Commission
Member—three positions (six-year terms of office)

Pension Benefit Guaranty Corporation
Director[125]

Railroad Retirement Board[126]
Member—three positions (five-year terms of office—Chair must be confirmed as both a member and as chair.)
Inspector General[127]

---

[125] The Director of the Pension Benefit Guaranty Corporation was established as a position to which appointments are made by the President, with the advice and consent of the Senate, by the Pension Protection Act of 2006 (P.L. 109-280, §411; 120 Stat. 935). The act provides that "[t]he Committee on Finance of the Senate and the Committee on Health, Education, Labor, and Pensions of the Senate shall have joint jurisdiction over the nomination of a person nominated by the President to fill [this position], and if one committee votes to order and report such a nomination, the other shall report within 30 calendar days, or be automatically discharged" (P.L. 109-280, §411(c)(1); 120 Stat. 935). The act also provides that the executive director at the time of enactment, "or any other individual, may serve as interim Director ... until an individual is appointed as Director" under the advice and consent process (P.L. 109-280, §411(d); 120 Stat. 936). The first nomination to this position was received by the Senate on May 3, 2007, and was referred as specified by law to the Senate Committees on Finance; and Health, Education, Labor, and Pensions.

[126] See also Committee on Homeland Security and Governmental Affairs (for inspector general position).

[127] Pursuant to a UC agreement, most IG nominations are referred sequentially to the committee with predominant jurisdiction over the particular IG's agency and then the Committee on Homeland Security and Governmental Affairs. For more information, see footnote 7.

* Nomination covered by S.Res. 116 with privileged status under a standing order of the Senate. See "112th Congress Standing Order on Nominations" for further explanation.

Part-Time Positions

Barry Goldwater Scholarship and Excellence in Education Foundation, Board of Trustees (political balance required)
*Member—eight (of 13 total) positions (six-year terms of office)

Corporation for National and Community Service, Board of Directors (political balance required)
*Member—15 positions (five-year terms of office)

Harry S. Truman Scholarship Foundation, Board of Trustees (political balance required)
*Member—eight (of 13 total) positions (six-year terms of office)

James Madison Memorial Fellowship Foundation, Board of Trustees (political balance required)
*Member—six (of 13 total) positions (six-year terms of office)

Legal Services Corporation Board of Directors (political balance required)
*Member—11 positions (three-year terms of office)

National Foundation on the Arts and the Humanities

National Council on the Arts
*Member—18 positions (of 25 total) positions (six-year terms of office)
National Council on the Humanities
*Member—26 positions (of 27 total) positions (six-year terms of office)

United States Institute of Peace, Board of Directors (political balance required)
*Chairman
*Vice Chairman
*Member—10 (of 15 total) positions (four-year terms of office)[128]

---

* Nomination covered by S.Res. 116 with privileged status under a standing order of the Senate. See "112th Congress Standing Order on Nominations" for further explanation.

Senate Committee on Homeland Security and Governmental Affairs

Full-Time Positions

Department of Commerce[129]
Director—Bureau of the Census (five-year term of office)[130]

Department of Homeland Security[131]
Secretary
Deputy Secretary
Under Secretary—Management
Under Secretary—National Protection and Programs[132]
Assistant Secretary—Policy
Assistant Secretary—U.S. Immigration and Customs Enforcement[133]
Assistant Secretary/Administrator—Transportation Security Administration[134]
Administrator—Federal Emergency Management Agency (FEMA)
Deputy Administrator—FEMA
Deputy Administrator—Protection and National Preparedness (FEMA)
*Chief Financial Officer[135]
General Counsel
Inspector General

---

[129] For other positions within the department, see also Committee on Banking, Housing, and Urban Affairs; Committee on Commerce, Science, and Transportation; Committee on Environment and Public Works; Committee on Finance; and Committee on the Judiciary.

[130] S. 679 (112th Congress) changed the term for the Director of the Bureau of the Census to a five-year term beginning in 2012, with a two-term limit.

[131] For other positions within the department, see also Committee on Commerce, Science, and Transportation; Committee on Homeland Security and Governmental Affairs; and Committee on the Judiciary. The Homeland Security Act authorizes not more than 12 assistant secretaries to be appointed by the President with the advice and consent of the Senate (6 U.S.C. §113).

[132] It could be argued that the Post-Katrina Emergency Management Reform Act of 2006 (Title VI of P.L. 109-295) abolished this position. For more information on this argument, see CRS Report RL33729, *Federal Emergency Management Policy Changes After Hurricane Katrina: A Summary of Statutory Provisions,* coordinated by Keith Bea. Notwithstanding this argument, the President submitted a nomination to this position on September 4, 2007; the nomination was referred to this committee then subsequently withdrawn by the President on December 19, 2007. On April 4, 2009, the President nominated Rand Beers to this position. He was subsequently confirmed by this committee on June 19, 2009.

[133] Nominees to this position are referred to the Committee on Homeland Security and Governmental Affairs and the Committee on the Judiciary pursuant to unanimous consent agreement of October 7, 2005. (Sen. Ted Stevens, "Sequential Referral of Nomination," remarks in the Senate, *Congressional Record*, vol. 151, October 7, 2005, p. 22639.) Within DHS this position is known as Director—U.S. Immigration and Customs Enforcement.

[134] Nominations to this position are referred sequentially to the Committee on Commerce, Science, and Transportation and the Committee on Homeland Security and Governmental Affairs.

[135] This chief financial officer (CFO) is one of the CFO positions covered by the Chief Financial Officers Act of 1990 (P.L. 101-576), as amended, that may be filled through appointment by the President, with the advice and consent of the Senate, or through designation by the President from among agency officials who have been confirmed by the Senate for other positions (31 U.S.C. §901(a)(1)).

Court Services and Offender Supervision Agency to the District of Columbia
Director (six-year term of office)

District of Columbia Court of Appeals (15-year terms of office)
Chief Judge
Associate Judges—8 positions

District of Columbia Superior Court (15-year terms of office)
Chief Judge
Associate Judges—sixty-one positions[136]

Superior Court of the District of Columbia (four-year terms of office)
United States Marshal[137]

Federal Labor Relations Authority (political balance required) Members—three positions
(five-year terms of office)
General Counsel (five-year term of office)

General Accountability Office
Comptroller General (15-year term of office)
Deputy Comptroller General[138]

General Services Administration
Administrator
Inspector General

Merit Systems Protection Board (political balance required)
Member—three positions (seven-year terms of office—Chair must be confirmed as both a
member and as chair.)

National Archives and Records Administration
Archivist

Office of the Director of National Intelligence (ODNI)
Inspector General of the Intelligence Community[139]

---

[136] The number of judges was changed from 59 (58 associate judges and one chief judge) to 62 (61 associate judges and one chief judge) by P.L. 108-207 (March 16, 2004).

[137] Title 28 U.S.C. §561(c) provides for the president to appoint a United States marshal for each judicial district of the United States and for the Superior Court of the District of Columbia. The nomination for the U.S. Marshal for the Superior Court of the District of Columbia is under the jurisdiction of the Senate Committee on Homeland Security and Governmental Affairs whereas the nominations for all other marshals are under the jurisdiction of the Senate Committee on the Judiciary.

[138] The term of the Deputy Comptroller General expires upon the appointment of a new Comptroller General, or when a successor is appointed (31 U.S.C. §703(b)). No one has been nominated to this office for at least 25 years.

* Nomination covered by S.Res. 116 with privileged status under a standing order of the Senate. See "112th Congress Standing Order on Nominations" for further explanation.

[139] Nominations to this position are referred sequentially to the Select Committee on Intelligence and the Committee on Homeland Security and Governmental Affairs pursuant to unanimous consent agreement of January 7, 2009, *Congressional Record*, vol. 155, part 1, p. 242.

Office of Government Ethics
Director (five-year term of office)

Office of Management and Budget (Executive Office of the President)
Director[140]
Deputy Director[141]
Deputy Director—Management
Administrator—Office of Federal Procurement Policy
Administrator—Office of Information and Regulatory Affairs
*Controller—Office of Federal Financial Management

Office of Personnel Management
Director (four-year term of office)
Deputy Director
Inspector General

Office of Special Counsel
Special Counsel (five-year term of office)

Postal Regulatory Commission (political balance required)
Commissioner—five positions (six-year terms of office)

Most Other Inspectors General[142]

Part-Time Positions

Federal Retirement Thrift Investment Board
*Member—five positions (four-year terms of office)

Special Panel on Appeals
Chair (six-year term of office)

United States Postal Service Board of Governors (political balance required)
Governor—nine positions (nine-year terms of office)

---

[140] On October 9, 2004, the Senate agreed to S.Res. 445 (108th Congress), which provided, in part, as follows: "The Committee on the Budget and the Committee on Homeland Security and Governmental Affairs shall have joint jurisdiction over the nominations of persons nominated by the President to fill the positions of Director and Deputy Director for Budget within the Office of Management and Budget, and if one committee votes to order reported such a nomination, the other must report within 30 calendar days session, or be automatically discharged" (§101(e)). Nominations to the positions of Director and Deputy Director of the Office of Management and Budget have been jointly referred to the two committees since the 109th Congress.

[141] Ibid.

* Nomination covered by S.Res. 116 with privileged status under a standing order of the Senate. See "112th Congress Standing Order on Nominations" for further explanation.

[142] Pursuant to a UC agreement, most IG nominations are referred sequentially to the committee with predominant jurisdiction over the particular IG's agency and then the Committee on Homeland Security and Governmental Affairs. For more information, see footnote 7.

* Nomination covered by S.Res. 116 with privileged status under a standing order of the Senate. See "112th Congress Standing Order on Nominations" for further explanation.

Senate Committee on Indian Affairs

Full-Time Positions

Department of Health and Human Services[143]
Director—Indian Health Service (four-year term of office)
*Commissioner—Administration for Native Americans

Department of the Interior[144]
Assistant Secretary—Indian Affairs
Chair—National Indian Gaming Commission (three-year term of office)
Special Trustee—American Indians

---

[143] For other positions within the department, see also Committee on Finance, Committee on Homeland Security and Governmental Affairs (for inspector general position), and Committee on Health, Education, Labor, and Pensions.

[144] For other positions within the department, see also Committee on Energy and Natural Resources, Committee on Environment and Public Works, and Committee on Homeland Security and Governmental Affairs (for inspector general position).

* Nomination covered by S.Res. 116 with privileged status under a standing order of the Senate. See p. 3 for further explanation.

Senate Select Committee on Intelligence

Full-Time Positions

Department of Homeland Security
Under Secretary for Intelligence and Analysis

Department of Justice
Assistant Attorney General—National Security Division[145]

Department of State
Assistant Secretary—Intelligence and Research[146]

Department of the Treasury
Assistant Secretary—Intelligence and Analysis

Central Intelligence Agency
Director
General Counsel
Inspector General

Office of the Director of National Intelligence (ODNI)
Director
Principal Deputy Director
Director—National Counterterrorism Center
General Counsel
Chief Information Officer
Inspector General of the Intelligence Community [147]

---

[145] Nominations to this position are referred sequentially to the Committee on the Judiciary and the Select Committee on Intelligence pursuant to Section 17(b)(1) of S.Res. 400 of the 94th Congress (as amended by §506(d) of P.L. 109-177 (March 9, 2006)). The applicable portion of the provision reads, "With respect to the confirmation of the Assistant Attorney General for National Security, or any successor position, the nomination of any individual by the President to serve in such position shall be referred to the Committee on the Judiciary and, if and when reported, to the select Committee for not to exceed 20 calendar days, except that in cases when the 20-day period expires while the Senate is in recess, the select Committee shall have 5 additional calendar days after the Senate reconvenes to report the nomination."

[146] Nominees to this position were initially referred to the Committee on Foreign Relations. The Senate agreed, by unanimous consent, that nominations for Assistant Secretary of State—Intelligence and Research be discharged from the Committee on Foreign Relations and that they be referred to the Committee on Intelligence. Sen. Mitch McConnell, "Referral of Discharged Nomination," remarks in the Senate, *Congressional Record*, vol. 152, part 8, June 14, 2006, p. 11186.

[147] Nominations to this position are referred sequentially to the Select Committee on Intelligence and the Committee on Homeland Security and Governmental Affairs pursuant to unanimous consent agreement of January 7, 2009, *Congressional Record*, vol. 155, part 1, p. 242.

Senate Committee on the Judiciary

Full-Time Positions

Department of Commerce[148]
Under Secretary—Intellectual Property/Director—U.S. Patent and Trademark Office

Department of Homeland Security[149]
Assistant Secretary—U.S. Immigration and Customs Enforcement[150]
Director—U.S. Citizenship and Immigration Services

Department of Justice[151]
Attorney General
Deputy Attorney General
Associate Attorney General
Assistant Attorney General—Antitrust Division
Assistant Attorney General—Civil Division
Assistant Attorney General—Civil Rights Division
Assistant Attorney General—Criminal Division
Assistant Attorney General—Environment and Natural Resources Division
*Assistant Attorney General—Legislative Affairs
Assistant Attorney General—National Security Division[152]
Assistant Attorney General—Office of Justice Programs
Assistant Attorney General—Office of Legal Counsel
Assistant Attorney General—Office of Legal Policy

---

[148] See also Committee on Banking, Housing, and Urban Affairs; Committee on Environment and Public Works; Committee on Finance; and Committee on Homeland Security and Governmental Affairs.

[149] For other positions within the department, see also Committee on Commerce, Science, and Transportation; Committee on Finance; and Committee on Homeland Security and Governmental Affairs. The Homeland Security Act authorizes not more than 12 assistant secretaries to be appointed by the President with the advice and consent of the Senate (6 U.S.C. §113).

[150] Nominees to this position are referred to the Committee on the Judiciary and the Committee on Homeland Security and Governmental Affairs pursuant to unanimous consent agreement of October 7, 2005. (Sen. Ted Stevens, "Sequential Referral of Nomination," remarks in the Senate, *Congressional Record*, vol. 151, part 17, October 7, 2005, p. 22639.) Within DHS this position is known as Director—U.S. Immigration and Customs Enforcement.

[151] Although the Department of Justice is included in the statute that provides presidentially appointed and Senate-confirmed chief financial officers for all of the major executive branch agencies (31 U.S.C. §901(a)(1)), this provision is superseded by 28 U.S.C. §507. The latter section provides that the Assistant Attorney General for Administration, appointed by the Attorney General with the approval of the President, shall be the CFO for the Department of Justice. See also Committee on Homeland Security and Governmental Affairs (for inspector general position).

[152] Nominations to this position are referred sequentially to the Committee on the Judiciary and the Select Committee on Intelligence pursuant to Section 17(b)(1) of S.Res. 400 of the 94th Congress (as amended by §506(d) of P.L. 109-177 (March 9, 2006)). The applicable portion of the provision reads, "With respect to the confirmation of the Assistant Attorney General for National Security, or any successor position, the nomination of any individual by the President to serve in such position shall be referred to the Committee on the Judiciary and, if and when reported, to the select Committee for not to exceed 20 calendar days, except that in cases when the 20-day period expires while the Senate is in recess, the select Committee shall have 5 additional calendar days after the Senate reconvenes to report the nomination."

* Nomination covered by S.Res. 116 with privileged status under a standing order of the Senate. See "112th Congress Standing Order on Nominations" for further explanation.

Assistant Attorney General—Tax Division
Administrator—Drug Enforcement Administration
Deputy Administrator—Drug Enforcement Administration
Director—Bureau of Alcohol, Tobacco, Firearms and Explosives
Director—Community Relations Service (four-year term of office)
Director—Federal Bureau of Investigation (10-year term of office)
Director—Office on Violence Against Women
Director—U.S. Marshals Service
Inspector General[153]
Solicitor General
Special Counsel—Immigration-Related Unfair Employment Practices (four-year term of office)
U.S. Attorney—93 positions (four-year terms of office)
U.S. Marshal—93 positions (four-year terms of office)[154]

Foreign Claims Settlement Commission
Chair—(three-year term of office; nominated from among commissioner members—See additional listing under part-time positions below.)

Office of National Drug Control Policy (Executive Office of the President)[155]
Director

Privacy and Civil Liberties Oversight Board[156]
Member—five positions (six-year term of office)

United States Circuit Court
Judges—179 positions (life tenure)

United States Court of Federal Claims
Judges—16 positions (15-year terms of office)

United States Court of International Trade (life tenure)
Judges—nine positions (political balance required)

United States District Courts[157]
Judges—677 positions (most are life tenure—These include four judges in three territorial courts, who are appointed to 10-year terms of office.)

---

[153] Pursuant to a UC agreement, most IG nominations are referred sequentially to the committee with predominant jurisdiction over the particular IG's agency and then the Committee on Homeland Security and Governmental Affairs. For more information, see footnote 7.

[154] Although the President may appoint separate U.S. attorneys and U.S. marshals for the District of Guam and the District of the Commonwealth of the Northern Mariana Islands (CNMI), this has never been done. One U.S. marshal and one U.S. attorney serve both Guam and the CNMI. See 48 U.S.C. §1821(b)(3-4).

[155] See also Committee on Health, Education, Labor, and Pensions for one other position within the agency.

[156] Established under Section 1061 of the Intelligence and Terrorism Prevention Act of 2004 (5 U.S.C. 601 note), P.L. 108-458 / 118 Stat. 3638. Positions include a chair, vice chair, and three additional members.

[157] The 677 district court judgeships consist of 663 permanent judgeships, 10 temporary judgeships, and four territorial court judgeships. In the districts with the 10 temporary judgeships, the seat lapses with the departure of a judge from that district at some particular time specified in statute unless Congress enacts legislation to extend the temporary judgeship or convert it to a permanent judgeship. A temporary judgeship in the Northern District of Ohio lapsed in (continued...)

United States Parole Commission[158]
Member—five positions (six-year term of office)

United States Sentencing Commission
Chair—(six-year term of office; nominated from among commission members.)[159]
Vice Chair—three positions (six-year terms of office; designated from among commission members.)

United States Supreme Court
Chief Justice—(life tenure)
Associate Justices—eight positions (life tenure)

Part-Time Positions

Foreign Claims Settlements Commission
*Member—three positions (three-year terms of office—One person is nominated to be the full-time chair of the commission along with two part-time members (22 U.S.C. 1622c(b)).

State Justice Institute, Board of Directors (political balance required)
*Director—11 positions (three-year terms of office, 42 U.S.C. 10708(a)(1)(c)).

United States Sentencing Commission (political balance required)
Commissioner—three positions (six-year terms of office)[160]

(...continued)

December 27, 2010.

[158] The President may designate one sitting member to be the chairman.

[159] There are seven voting members appointed through the advice and consent process. The chair and three vice chairs are full-time positions per 28 U.S.C. 992. The other three positions are part-time positions as described in 28 U.S.C. 992(c).

* Nomination covered by S.Res. 116 with privileged status under a standing order of the Senate. See "112th Congress Standing Order on Nominations" for further explanation.

[160] Three commissioners serve part-time as described in 28 U.S.C. 992(c). The other three members of the Commission are the chair and three vice chairs who serve full-time per 28 U.S.C. 992.

Senate Committee on Rules and Administration

Full-Time Positions

Architect of the Capitol
Architect

Election Assistance Commission (political balance required)
Commissioner—four positions (four-year terms of office)

Federal Election Commission (political balance required)
Commissioners—six positions (six-year terms of office)

Government Printing Office
Public Printer

Library of Congress
Librarian

Senate Committee on Small Business and Entrepreneurship

Full-Time Positions

Small Business Administration[161]
Administrator
Deputy Administrator
Chief Counsel for Advocacy
Inspector General[162]

---

[161] See also Committee on Homeland Security and Governmental Affairs (for inspector general position).

[162] Pursuant to a UC agreement, most IG nominations are referred sequentially to the committee with predominant jurisdiction over the particular IG's agency and then the Committee on Homeland Security and Governmental Affairs. For more information, see footnote 7.

Senate Committee on Veterans' Affairs

Full-Time Positions

Department of Labor[163]
Assistant Secretary—Veterans' Employment and Training Service[164]

Department of Veterans Affairs[165]
Secretary
Deputy Secretary
Under Secretary—Benefits (four-year term of office)
Under Secretary—Health (four-year term of office)
Under Secretary—Memorial Affairs
*Assistant Secretary—Congressional and Legislative Affairs
Assistant Secretary—Information and Technology
Assistant Secretary—Policy and Planning
Chair—Board of Veterans' Appeals (six-year term of office)
*Chief Financial Officer[166]
General Counsel
Inspector General[167]

United States Court of Appeals for Veterans Claims
Judge—37 positions (15-year terms of office)

---

[163] For other positions in this department, see also Committee on Homeland Security and Governmental Affairs (for inspector general position) and Committee on Health, Education, Labor, and Pensions.

[164] Nominations to this position are referred jointly to the Committee on Health, Education, Labor, and Pensions and the Committee on Veterans' Affairs pursuant to a unanimous consent agreement of May 24, 2005. Sen. Bill Frist, "Joint Referral," remarks in the Senate, *Congressional Record*, vol. 151, part 8, May 24, 2005, p. 10958.

[165] See also Committee on Homeland Security and Governmental Affairs (for inspector general position).

[166] This chief financial officer (CFO) is one of the CFO positions covered by the Chief Financial Officers Act of 1990 (P.L. 101-576), as amended, that may be filled through appointment by the President, with the advice and consent of the Senate, or through designation by the President from among agency officials who have been confirmed by the Senate for other positions (31 U.S.C. §901(a)(1)).

[167] Pursuant to a UC agreement, most IG nominations are referred sequentially to the committee with predominant jurisdiction over the particular IG's agency and then the Committee on Homeland Security and Governmental Affairs. For more information, see footnote 7.

* Nomination covered by S.Res. 116 with privileged status under a standing order of the Senate. See "112th Congress Standing Order on Nominations" for further explanation.

Appendix. Presidential Appointee Positions That No Longer Require Senate Confirmation Per P.L. 112-166, the Presidential Appointment Efficiency and Streamlining Act of 2011

Table A-1. Positions That No Longer Require Senate Confirmation Per P.L. 112-166

(positions listed by Senate Committee of Jurisdiction)

Agriculture, Nutrition and Forestry

Assistant Secretary for Administration, Department of Agriculture	Rural Utilities Service Administrator, Department of Agriculture
Directors (7), Commodity Credit Corporation	

Armed Services

Members (6), National Security Education Board	Director, Selective Service

Banking, Housing and Urban Affairs

Administrator, Community Development Financial Institution Fund, Department of the Treasury	Assistant Secretary for Public Affairs, Department of Housing and Urban Development
Members (2), Council of Economic Advisers	

Commerce, Science, and Transportation[a]

Deputy Administrator, Federal Aviation Administration	Chief Scientist, National Oceanic and Atmospheric Administration
Assistant Secretary for Administration, Department of Transportation[b]	Assistant Secretary for Budget and Programs, Department of Transportation[c]
Administrator, St. Lawrence Seaway Development Corporation	

Environment and Public Works

Alternate Federal Co-Chairman, Appalachian Regional Commission	Commissioners (7), Mississippi River Corporation

Finance

Assistant Secretary for Public Affairs, Department of Treasury	Treasurer of the United States
Assistant Secretary for Management, Department of Treasury[d]	

Foreign Relations

Assistant Secretary for Public Affairs, Department of State	Assistant Administrator for Management, U.S. Agency for International Development
Assistant Secretary for Administration, Department of State	

Health, Education, Labor and Pensions[e]

Assistant Secretary for Management, Department of Education	Assistant Secretary for Public Affairs, Department of Labor
Commissioner, Education Statistics, Department of Education	Members (15), National Council on Disability
Assistant Secretary for Public Affairs, Department of Health and Human Services	Members (24), National Science Foundation
Managing Directors (2), Corporation for National and Community Service	Members (15), National Board of Education Sciences
Assistant Secretary for Administration and Management, Department of Labor	Members (10), National Institute for Literacy Advisory Board
Director of the Women's Bureau, Department of Labor	Members (20), National Museum and Library Services Board, National Foundation of the Arts and Humanities

Homeland Security and Governmental Affairs

Director, Office of Counternarcotics Enforcement, Department of Homeland Security	Chief Medical Officer, Department of Homeland Security
Director, Office for Domestic Preparedness, Federal Emergency Management Administration, Department of Homeland Security	Administrator, U.S. Fire Administration, Department of Homeland Security
Assistant Secretary for Health Affairs, Department of Homeland Security	Assistant Secretary for Legislative Affairs, Department of Homeland Security
Assistant Administrator for Grant Programs, Federal Emergency Management Administration, Department of Homeland Security	Assistant Secretary for Public Affairs, Department of Homeland Security

Indian Affairs

Commissioner, Office of Navajo and Hopi Indian Relocation	Members (13), Board of Trustees, Institute of American Indian and Alaska Native Culture and Arts Development

Judiciary

Director, Bureau of Justice Statistics, Department of Justice	Deputy Director, Office of National Drug Control Policy, Executive Office of the President
Director, Bureau of Justice Assistance, Department of Justice	Deputy Director, Demand Reduction, Office of National Drug Control Policy, Executive Office of the President
Director, National Institute of Justice, Department of Justice	Deputy Director, Supply Reduction, Office of National Drug Control Policy, Executive Office of the President
Director, Office for Victims of Crime, Department of Justice	Deputy Director, State, Local, and Tribal Affairs, Office of National Drug Control Policy, Executive Office of the President
Administrator, Office of Juvenile Justice and Delinquency Prevention, Department of Justice	

Veterans' Affairs

Assistant Secretary for Management, Department of Veterans Affairs	Assistant Secretary for Operations, Security, and Preparedness, Department of Veterans Affairs
Assistant Secretary for Human Resources and Administration, Department of Veterans Affairs	Assistant Secretary for Public and Intergovernmental Affairs, Department of Veterans Affairs

Source: Congressional Research Service, based upon the lists provided in the *Congressional Record* upon introduction of S. 679 (*Congressional Record,* vol. 157, part 44 (March 30, 2011), pp. 1985-1990). Changes made in committee markup were identified through *Congressional Quarterly* and are available at http://www.cq.com/pdf/ 3852080. Committee jurisdiction was determined based upon the list provided in the *Congressional Record* upon the bill's introduction, as well as examination of past referrals of nominations in the Legislative Information System's nominations database. See also CRS Report R41872, *Presidential Appointments, the Senate's Confirmation Process, and Changes Made in the 112th Congress*, by Maeve P. Carey, in which this table first appeared.

Notes: In addition to eliminating advice and consent requirements for the positions listed here, P.L. 112-166 also makes some other changes. In the Department of Defense, the authorized number of Assistant Secretaries is reduced from 16 to 14. The two that would be eliminated in accordance with that reduction would be the Assistant Secretary of Defense for Networks and Information Integration and the Assistant Secretary of Defense for Public Affairs. Within 180 days of the enactment of P.L. 112-166, the Secretary of Defense is required to report to the appropriate congressional committees his plan for establishing positions that would fulfill the functions of those two Assistant Secretary positions, but they could not be subject to Senate confirmation or at the Assistant Secretary level. Another change made by the passage of P.L. 112-166 is that the Director of the Bureau of the Census would have a five-year term, beginning in 2012, with a two-term limit. Additionally, for the positions of Governor and Alternate Governor for the African Development Bank, Asian Development Bank, and African Development Fund, the President can nominate an individual with the advice and consent of the Senate, or he can designate an individual to fill those positions from among individuals serving in positions that are already, independently, subject to advice and consent of the Senate.

a. An additional 319 National Oceanic and Atmospheric Administration Officer Corps positions are typically referred to the Committee on Commerce, Science, and Transportation. These are included in P.L. 112-166 and will no longer be considered by the Senate. Nominations for the NOAA Officer Corps are sometimes considered *en bloc*, or in a list that receives a single vote.

b. P.L. 112-166 requires the Assistant Secretary for Administration to be appointed by the Secretary with the approval of the President.

c. It appears that the Assistant Secretary for Budget and Programs also serves as the CFO in the Department of Transportation. P.L. 112-166 eliminates the advice and consent requirement for the Assistant Secretary position, but the CFO position will still require advice and consent. The CFO position for Transportation is included in P.L. 112-166.

d. It appears that the Assistant Secretary for Management also serves as the CFO in the Department of the Treasury. P.L. 112-166 eliminates the advice and consent requirement for the Assistant Secretary position, but the CFO position will still require advice and consent. The CFO position for Treasury is included in P.L. 112-166.

e. The advice and consent requirements for an additional 2,536 Public Health Services Officer Corps positions have been eliminated as well by P.L. 112-166. These nominations are typically non-controversial and are considered by the Senate *en bloc*, with the Senate considering a large number of nominees and casting a single vote for the entire list. The list may include dozens or even hundreds of nominees.

Author Contact Information

Christopher M. Davis
Analyst on Congress and the Legislative Process
cmdavis@crs.loc.gov, 7-0656

Jerry W. Mansfield
Information Research Specialist

Acknowledgment

This report was originally authored by Henry B. Hogue, analyst in American National Government, and Maureen Bearden, information research specialist. The listed authors would like to acknowledge the assistance that CRS colleagues Maureen Bearden, Maeve P. Carey, and Henry B. Hogue provided during the updating of this report.